You Did
What?

You Did
What?

The Biggest Mistakes Professionals Make

Fifth Edition

Kim Zoller · Kerry Preston

Brown Books Publishing Group
Dallas, Texas

You Did What?
The Biggest Mistakes Professionals Make
Fifth Edition

Brown Books Publishing Group
16250 Knoll Trail Drive, Suite 205
Dallas, Texas 75248
www.BrownBooks.com
(972) 381-0009

A New Era in Publishing™

ISBN: 978-1-61254-027-6
Library of Congress Control Number 2011934574

Printing in the United States
10 9 8 7 6

Second Edition © 2002 by IDImage, Inc.
Third Edition © 2006 by Kim Zoller and Kerry Preston
Fourth Edition © 2007 by Kim Zoller and Kerry Preston

Contents

Acknowledgments

This book was started many years ago with the simple goal of offering something that wasn't on the market. We wanted to provide a quick and easy reference guide for a business community that didn't have time to read an in-depth etiquette book.

Many thanks to our wonderful clients and seminar participants for asking valid questions. Through their active participation, this book was written with them and their colleagues in mind.

We want to thank our team for their input and excitement regarding this project. We have an amazing support team and could not have accomplished this without them.

We thank the creativity of Andrew Grossman and Roger Pennwill for their wonderful cartoons.

We thank and acknowledge our husbands, Tim Reinagel and Keith Lebowitz, and our children—Ben, Sam, Luke, Wes, and Nate—who gave us many hours of quiet to let us complete this book. We also thank our parents, Harriet and David Whiting and Kathleen Preston for all of their support.

Introduction

"There is no accomplishment so easy to acquire as
politeness, and none more profitable."
—George Bernard Shaw

Successful people leave nothing undone. To them, every detail matters. In many instances, success is determined by interpersonal skills rather than technical skills. After analyzing the records of ten thousand people, the Carnegie Institute of Technology concluded that 15 percent of job success is due to technical training, intellect, and job skills and 85 percent of job success is due to personality factors. In other words, job success is determined, in greatest measure, by one's ability to deal with other people successfully.

Harvard University's Bureau of Vocational Guidance conducted a study of thousands of men and women who had been fired. The study showed that for every one person who lost a job for failure to do work, two people lost jobs for failure to deal successfully with other people.

Setting yourself apart in today's highly competitive business environment takes thought and planning. To be a truly professional and successful individual in the workplace, not only must a person have excellent job skills, he or she must have excellent people skills as well.

There is nothing worse than walking into a situation and not knowing how it should be handled. Professionalism is expected and respected. Lack of professionalism can ruin your career. *You Did What?* is about making sure that your mistakes do not get in the way of your career. Nothing goes unnoticed. Don't bring your career to a halt without even realizing it. Walk into every situation feeling confident. Don't ever be in a situation in which you are recounting an interaction and have someone say, "You did *what?*"

Big Mistake

1

Forgetting to Stay One Step Ahead

"Behavior is a mirror in which everyone displays his own image."

—Johann Wolfgang von Goethe

People tend to focus on small things that can affect your future. Impressions are made in seconds. Most of the time, these impressions determine the outcome of a situation before the actual interaction begins. We've all heard the saying, "You don't get a second chance to make a first impression."

Most businesspeople determine if they want to do business with you based on these first impressions. By planning ahead, you can decide what you want your image to be and what impressions you would like to leave with them. This gives others every opportunity to do business with you, hire you, and be loyal to you.

——————————— On the Side ———————————

"Recently we were selecting a vendor to furnish our new office. We couldn't believe the treatment we received. Some vendors acted as though they were doing us a favor. Others arrived a few minutes late to our first meeting. We hired the vendor who had the most professional people—the people who treated us well and acted as though they were thrilled to be with us. They were willing to do whatever it took to make us happy. It's a pity that the other vendors overlooked the possibilities. It turned out to be $100,000 worth of business."

—A San Francisco law firm

Think about the people you know who are successful and professional.

Ask Yourself These Crucial Questions
- What makes them professional?
- What did I learn from them that can help me become more professional?
- How do I want people to perceive me?
- What image do I want to project?

There are three basic components that contribute to a person's impression of us:
- 7 percent of an impression comes from the words we use
- 38 percent of an impression comes from the way we sound (our intonation and enunciation)
- 55 percent of an impression comes from our nonverbal messages (our body language)

These components determine how others perceive us and also how they react to us. Being one step ahead means leaving nothing to chance. You must perfect the details of how you present yourself.

Tips

Your goal in business should be to give people the opportunity to actually hear what you have to say. You lose your competitive advantage when people become distracted by aspects of your appearance or by behaviors that you can easily change.

- Always stay "one step ahead" of your competition.
- Be on time.
- Be dressed appropriately.
- Be dressed for where you *want* to be in your career, not for your current position.
- Be informed.
- Be interested, not interesting.
- Use appropriate language.
- Be personable, not personal.
- Respond yes or no, verbally or in written form, when you are invited to a function. People remember.
- Follow up and follow through.
- It is better to "under-promise" and "over-deliver."
- Send handwritten thank-you notes. (For more information, see chapter 3, Being Sloppy with Written and Verbal Correspondence.)

Attitude is everything! As Norman Vincent Peale once said, "Any fact facing us is not as important as our attitude toward it, for that determines our success or failure."

Big Mistake

2

Using Body Language Improperly

"What you are shouts so loud in my ears,
I cannot hear what you say."

—Ralph Waldo Emerson

The meaning behind body language is never entirely clear. However, being aware and understanding the general guidelines regarding body language will provide you with powerful ammunition to convey the nonverbal messages you wish to send. Remember, body language is accountable for an astounding 55 percent of the impression you make during a business meeting.

During the next week, observe the body language and gestures of the people around you—in a meeting, on an elevator, or while driving or dining.

Ask Yourself These Crucial Questions

- What did I notice?
- What perceptions do I have and what impressions have I formed?

Body Language Specifics

Handshakes

Your handshake must be firm. A firm handshake communicates confidence.

- The web between your thumb and forefinger should meet the web of the other person's hand.
- Extend your hand immediately at the beginning and end of an interaction.
- Stand when you are shaking hands.

———————————— On the Side ————————————

"I was having a terrible experience buying a car. No one was taking me seriously, which was very frustrating. A friend of mine referred me to a dealership where he had been treated well. I decided this was the last place I would visit before I resorted to the Internet. When I walked in, an extremely professional and polished gentleman in a suit came up and greeted me. He made confident eye contact, smiled, put out his hand, introduced himself by name, and welcomed me to the dealership. I was sold. The salespeople at the two top-notch dealerships I visited previously had given me fishy handshakes and made no eye contact. It was as though they were saying that they didn't want my business."

—Female advertising agency executive

Eye Contact

- Make eye contact immediately when meeting a person.
- Maintain eye contact throughout your conversation.
- Do not look at the ground, even if you are nervous.
- When you ask or answer a question, make and maintain eye contact.
- When you shake hands at the end of the interaction, maintain eye contact.

Posture

- Do not slouch when sitting or standing. This type of posture is often associated with a lack of confidence.

Arm and Hand Position

- Do not put your hands in your pockets.
- Keep your hands in view, either on your lap or at your side.
- Do not cross your arms. This behavior is often misinterpreted as anger, lack of interest, or boredom.
- Do not fidget with your pens, hair, rings, and so forth.
- Do not point your fingers or make a fist. These actions may make others feel intimidated.
- Always cover your mouth when coughing or yawning.

Tips

Remember that even before you begin to speak, people focus on your body language. Fifty-five percent of the impression you make is nonverbal. Even if you don't feel confident in a situation, others must think you are. How people initially perceive you sets the stage for all the interactions that follow.

Be careful. Make sure that the impression you send is a positive one. A negative impression can be damaging to your image and is very hard to overcome.

Big Mistake

Being Sloppy with Written and Verbal Correspondence

"Simple speech is the best and truest eloquence."
—Ralph Waldo Emerson

Positive personal interactions allow you to build a rapport with others that will guarantee your success. Knowing when to write a note or make a phone call is priceless. Time is limited, but if you don't take the time when "the time is right," you will spend more of it later. Success in building relationships is in the details.

On the Side

"Recently we met with a prospective client. We noticed a bulletin board at the side of his desk that had a variety of little note cards on it. Noticing that we were looking at it, our client said, 'Everything being equal, I do business with vendors who send me notes thanking me for my time and my business.' Handwritten notes do make a difference."

—Image Dynamics executives

Ask Yourself These Crucial Questions

- When was the last time a vendor or salesperson wrote me a note to say thank you?
- Did it make an impression on me?
- If I could get my desired result by taking five minutes to do something, would I?

Written Correspondence

It is acceptable to put a business card in a handwritten note only when the recipient has asked for a card and is expecting one. When you include a business card that has not been asked for, you make a very personal touch impersonal. This can damage the rapport you are trying to build.

When writing a handwritten note, you will want to use fold-over notepaper or note cards that measure at least 3½ x 5 inches. These are known as "informal notes." Plain white or cream informal notes are available at all stationery stores. Stationery that is engraved, thermographed, embossed, or printed adds a personal touch.

Types of written correspondence include personal letters, condolence letters, letters of congratulations, thank-you notes, reference letters, letters of introduction, and letters of greeting.

Handwritten notes should be written:

- When someone takes the time to meet with you
- Following any type of interview—internal or external
- When you have been a guest at a cocktail or dinner party
- When you have been invited to someone's home

- When you receive a gift
- When customers or associates have been promoted
- When customers or associates have had a death in their family
- When customers or associates celebrate a marriage, the birth or adoption of a child, or receive some special recognition

Remember, to be an effective writer you should:
- Have a strong sense of purpose about a letter before writing it
- Limit your letter to one page
- Get to the point early (within the first two sentences)
- Emphasize the reader's perspective (ask yourself how your message will benefit them)
- Never write in anger
- Be personable (don't use a form letter, as it may not fully apply)
- Never send a letter with any hand deletions or corrections
- End with an action item that suggests the next step
- Also handwrite the envelope of a handwritten note

Examples of Written Correspondence
A "Nice to Meet You" Note

Dear John,
It was so nice meeting you yesterday. I appreciate you taking the time; I know you are extremely busy. Your work sounds so interesting—I would love to hear

more about it. I look forward to seeing you at the next association meeting.

Sincerely yours,
Kim Zoller

A "Thank You" Note

Dear Matt,
Thank you for giving me the opportunity to work with you. I know you have a choice of where you purchase your printing and I appreciate you choosing us. Please do not hesitate to call if you need anything or have any questions. I will follow up with you in a couple of weeks.

All the best,
Kerry Preston

An "Internal Interview" Note

Dear Mike,
As you know, I really enjoy working here and I appreciate you considering me for the opening in your department. Every new challenge is exciting and I am looking forward to the opportunity.

I will follow up with you next week as you suggested. Thank you again for considering me.

Sincerely,
John Smith

An "External Interview" Note

Dear Mike,

It was a pleasure meeting you to discuss the sales position. I have such a high regard for [name of company] and I look forward to the opportunity to work with you and your team. Thank you for considering me.

I will follow up with you next week as you suggested.

Sincerely yours,

Mary Smith

A "Thanks for Having Me Over" Note

Dear Jane,

What a wonderful evening! Thank you for inviting me to your holiday party. I enjoyed meeting everyone and spending some time with you. I look forward to seeing you soon.

Warmest regards,

Kerry Preston

A "My Condolences" Note

Dear Susan,

I was so sorry to hear about your mother. This must be a difficult time for you. I want you to know that you and your family are in my thoughts.

With deepest sympathy,

Kim Zoller

Verbal Correspondence

It's not only what you say but how you say it. Technology will never take the place of a live voice. Make the most of every opportunity you have to connect with people. These connections help you build your professional reputation.

Examples of Verbal Correspondence

An Introductory Phone Call

Introductory telephone calls should always start with: "Susan, this is [your name] with [company name]. Do you have a moment?" Or, "Susan, this is [your name] with [company name]. [Referral source] suggested that I give you a call. Do you have a moment?"

If the people you call say that they are busy and will return your call later, respond by saying, "If I don't hear from you by Wednesday, may I call you back? Thank you." Suggest a time within the next couple of days. People get busy, so put yourself in charge of the situation.

A Verbal Condolence

"Susan, hello, it's John Smith. I don't want to take too much of your time; I just want you to know how sorry I am to hear about your mother. Please call me if you need anything."

A Verbal Thank-You

"Susan, hi, it's Kim Zoller. Thank you so much for your help on the project. I appreciate your time and help. Please let me know when I can return the favor."

A Verbal Acknowledgement

"Susan, hi, it's Kerry Preston. I was thinking about you today and wanted to wish you a happy birthday. Have a wonderful day."

Responding to an Invitation Marked RSVP

The rules for RSVPs pertain to both business and social functions (i.e., meetings, seminars, after-hour parties, etc.). When an invitation asks for an RSVP, you must send a reply either in writing or verbally. It doesn't matter whether you are accepting or declining the invitation. Some invitations may be marked with something to the effect of "RSVP only if declining." In these cases, you should respond only if you cannot attend.

Tips

- A verbal or written response should be made within one week if an RSVP is requested.
- The RSVP should be made by phone if a telephone number is included with the invitation.
- Once you have made your RSVP, the host must be made aware of any changes as soon as possible.
- Do not send someone in your place if you are unable to attend.
- Do not bring a guest unless the invitation is addressed specifically to you and a guest.

If you fail to RSVP or you respond yes and do not attend, you can be sure that your host will remember. Negative impressions are difficult to overcome and can be extremely costly in the long run.

Both written and verbal correspondence are crucial in cultivating relationships and gaining a competitive advantage. They should be looked at as opportunities for you to make favorable impressions and to help you stay one step ahead of the competition.

Big Mistake

Breaking the Rules
for Introductions

"Civility costs nothing and buys everything."
—Lady Mary Wortley Montagu

Knowing "the whos and whens" of introductions is a key component in maintaining your competitive advantage. Many people draw blanks or forget names when they are trying to make introductions. There are many reasons for this, but often in a business setting it is because they feel overwhelmed with the responsibility of leading the introduction process.

Ask Yourself These Crucial Questions

- Have I ever been in a situation in which someone did not extend his or her hand for a handshake when I first met them? Did it make me feel uncomfortable?
- Do I introduce myself by name and with a handshake when I first meet a business acquaintance?
- Do I introduce the others around me?

─────────────── **On the Side** ───────────────

"It was a Sunday and I went to the mall. Dressed in jeans and a T-shirt, I did not look the way I look during the week. I saw a client with whom I had a good relationship but had not seen in years. I walked up to her with a big smile on my face and said, 'Hi. How are you?' She smiled and gave me a big hug. As she stepped back from the hug, she looked at me apologetically and said, 'I'm so sorry. Please tell me your name again.' From that moment on, I decided that it is best to introduce myself in any situation where someone may not be able to remember me, what we did together, or my name."

—New Jersey sales representative

Tips

If there is the slightest chance that someone may not be able to remember your name or how he or she knows you, make it a policy to put out your hand and introduce yourself immediately. This will put the other person at ease right away.

Introductions are important. Always remember to introduce yourself and others in your group. When you introduce yourself, make sure you state your full name and your company name (e.g., "Hello. I'm Kim Zoller with Image Dynamics. Nice to meet you."). If there are others in your group, introduce them as well (e.g., "This is Joann Smith and John Wise. They are also with Image Dynamics.").

In most instances when making introductions, you should mention the most important person first (i.e., the person to whom you want to show greatest respect or honor). Phrases like "I'd like you to meet . . . ," "Have you met . . . ," and "This is . . . ," may be helpful.

Examples
Introducing someone to your boss:
    "John, I'd like you to meet my wife, Susan. Susan, John is my boss."

Introducing someone to your customer:
    "Kerry, have you met my manager, Joe? Joe, Kerry works with [company name]."

Introducing several people to your customer:
    "Lisa, this is our accounting department. Everyone, Lisa is with [company name]."

It is all right to mention the least important person first if you use the phrase, "[Name of person], I'd like to introduce you to . . ."

Examples
    "Susan, I'd like to introduce you to my manager, Joe. Joe, Susan is my wife."
    "Joe, I'd like to introduce you to Kerry, with [company name]. Kerry, Joe is my manager."

Big Mistake

5

Making Small Talk and Networking Inappropriately

Bob couldn't figure out why his phone never rang
after handing out 1000 business cards in two days.

"Talk to a man about himself and
he will listen for hours."

—Benjamin Disraeli

Knowing how to network and make appropriate small talk can open doors that determine lifetime success. If you are not networking today, you may be missing some wonderful opportunities. Be prepared and equipped with the proper protocol.

Ask Yourself These Crucial Questions

- What topics are appropriate when conversing during networking situations?
- Do I know what I want to achieve at every networking event?
- While I am making small talk with someone, do I know what I am trying to get out of the interaction?

Be prepared for any situation in which you may meet someone or make a contact that could be beneficial to you. Always stay "on your toes" so that you do not lose any opportunities.

─────────────── On the Side ───────────────

"As I am writing this, I am sitting on an airplane. The person sitting next to me just happens to be someone who makes decisions for his company about training. It reminds me of another time I was sitting on an airplane, tired and desperate to get home. I did not want to talk to anyone. I was sitting next to a lady who asked me what I did for a living. Luckily I put a smile on my face and answered her cordially. Before I knew it, she was telling me that she was a top executive for a Fortune 100 company. Based on that networking opportunity, my company is now doing a lot of work for her and her team."

—Corporate trainer

Networking and Small Talk Specifics

You should always prepare for small talk and networking opportunities ahead of time. You will find the following ideas helpful.

- Plan three items or stories to share.
- Prepare four generic questions to ask. Make sure they are open-ended questions that cannot be answered with a simple yes or no.
- Use the newspaper, an experience, current events, or books and movies as subjects.
- Think about each item or issue carefully. Consider the ramifications a topic might have, questions it might generate, or opinions that others might have on it.

Body Language While Networking

"Actions speak louder than words." Sound familiar? Make sure your body language sends a message about how happy you are to be there.

- Stand confidently and extend your hand immediately when meeting or greeting someone.
- Eye contact must be maintained while shaking hands and talking to someone. Don't worry about what others are doing. Stay focused.
- Your posture must be tall and confident. If you slouch, you send others the message that you lack confidence, that you are not friendly, or that you are unapproachable.
- Keep your arms uncrossed, even if you are more comfortable crossing them. Crossed arms may send a message of boredom or defensiveness.

Most people are uncomfortable making small talk. Having a plan in mind before you go out will make the situation easier for you. The following is a list of "Small Talk Don'ts" that will keep you from offending someone. We've included some "Small Talk Dos" as well.

These small talk tips can be used in all business situations. They will help you initiate conversations and open doors of opportunity.

Small Talk Don'ts

Avoid getting into discussions on:
- Politics
- Religion

- Sexism
- Racist or ethnic comments
- Sexual orientation
- Salary
- Gossip
- Negativism
- Private matters
- Private family matters

While a discussion may center on something that is of little or no consequence to you, the topic may be of great importance to the person with whom you are having the discussion. Always keep in mind that not all people think or feel as you do.

Other Small Talk Don'ts

- Giving too much personal information
- Giving an overabundance of detail
- Interrogating rather than conversing
- Interrupting the other person
- Complaining
- Trying to "one-up" the other person
- Glancing around the room while someone is conversing with you

Small Talk Dos

Safe topics for conversations include:

- Career background
- Achievements and goals
- Hobbies and leisure activities
- Community involvement
- Entertainment, such as favorite movies and books

- Current events (as long as they are not controversial)
- Family (as long as the other person brings it up first—don't get too personal)

Other Small Talk Dos
- Shake hands firmly and introduce yourself
- Smile
- Keep a positive attitude
- Be aware of the other person's time
- Listen carefully

Ready . . . Set . . . Talk

"Hi. I'm Kim Zoller with Image Dynamics. It's nice to meet you. This looks like an interesting meeting. How long have you been involved in the association?"

Don't continue speaking. Listen to the response to your question.

"How did you get started in your business?"

Don't continue speaking. Listen to the response to your question.

"What do you enjoy most about what you do?"

Don't continue speaking. Listen to the response to your question.

"What significant changes have you seen in your industry through the years?"

Don't continue speaking. Listen to the response to your question.

"What do you see as upcoming trends?"

Don't continue speaking. Listen to the response to your question.

Tips

- Take a deep breath and relax. Figure out what your body is saying.
- Wear your name tag on your *right* lapel.
- Hold your drink or food in your left hand so you can shake with your right hand.
- Use a mint if you need one. Do not chew gum.
- Hand out business cards only when you are specifically asked for them. Ask for a business card in return and follow up.
- Make eye contact before you start the conversation.
- Extend your hand and introduce yourself, giving your full name (and your company name when applicable).
- Ask questions: Be interested, not interesting. If someone thinks that you are only interested in talking about yourself, you will come across as conceited and disinterested in anyone else. You will also seem less interesting than you really are.
- Use the person's name throughout the conversation, but be careful not to overuse it.
- Be careful when you compliment another person. Compliment them only if you sincerely feel that way.
- Wait to see if they bring up personal issues before you start talking about them.
- Never discuss personal problems. Negativity is always a reflection of your personality.
- Talk about a relevant article you have read recently or a seminar you have attended that you feel might enhance the conversation.
- Keep abreast of world events.

36

- Keep a log of all of the contacts you have made.
- Keep track of all of your discussions and any other pertinent information (i.e., what you were wearing, specifics about each of the people you met, family, hobbies, etc.).

Creating a Lasting Impression

- Gather business cards and follow up.
- Send a handwritten "Nice to Meet You" note.
- Never promise something that you cannot deliver. People will remember forever.
- If you see an article about someone you know or have met, cut out the article and send it to them with a note. You would be amazed at what an impression this makes.
- The world is a very small place. Once you have burned a bridge, you may have burned many. News travels fast and your reputation is all you have.

Big Mistake

6

Forgetting Names

"Who steals my purse steals trash. . . . But he that
filches from me my good name robs me of that which
not enriches him and makes me poor indeed."

—William Shakespeare, *Othello*

Remembering someone's name is one of the most powerful tools for networking and building relationships. There is nothing greater than the sound of one's own name. Normally people are so focused on what they are going to say when they meet someone, they either don't hear that person's name or they just don't remember it. Many people are offended and take it very personally when their names are not remembered. The first or second time you forget someone's name, you should apologize and ask for their name again. If his or her name is still a problem for you, make sure you get the name from someone else.

Remembering names does matter.

───────────── **On the Side** ─────────────

"Every month I go to a vendor breakfast. It never seems to fail that I run into Joe, the one person who never remembers my name. Joe does business with my company and he has had to deal with me.

Recently I was promoted to manager of training and development. In my new position, I am responsible for making decisions on which vendors the company uses. I have decided to look for someone other than Joe who can do what he does. It's amazing how his lack of interest in me has made me want to look for someone else."

—UPS executive

Ask Yourself These Crucial Questions
- How do I feel when someone remembers my name?
- Am I uncomfortable when I forget another person's name?
- When people remember my name at a meeting, event, or workshop, am I more inclined to think about doing business with them?

Tips
- When you are being introduced, focus on the other person's name, not on what you want to say after the introduction.
- Repeat the person's name immediately (e.g., "John, it is so nice to meet you.").
- Visualize the name (e.g., try to see it written across the person's forehead).
- Use the person's name throughout the conversation. Be careful you don't repeat it so much that it becomes awkward.
- Try to associate this person's name with an object or another person with the same name (e.g., you might associ-

ate Kim Zoller with Kim Basinger; Ronald Smith with Ronald Regan; Mr. Campbell with Campbell's Soup; etc.).

Many of the above strategies for remembering are not easy to learn. However, with time, practice, and awareness, you will be able to use them effectively. The ability to remember names is a powerful tool. It will help you in your quest to increase your competitive advantage.

Big Mistake

7

Lacking Technology Etiquette

"E-mail is a unique communication vehicle for a lot of reasons. However, e-mail is not a substitute for direct interaction."

—Bill Gates

In every seminar, we ask people to tell us what offends them at work. Lately the majority of stories have involved technology (problems with e-mails, voice mails, etc.). These updated modes of communication have become informal ways for us to keep in touch with one another and to help get our messages across quickly. Despite the fact that technology has changed the way people look at communication, it has not changed the reactions that people have with regard to the messages they receive.

In today's hectic business environments, time has become an expensive commodity. Time-saving tools such as e-mail and voice mail increase the speed of our communications. While these technologies are a less formal mode for communication, it is important to remember that your effectiveness can be lost if you are too informal. Keep in mind that you are always creating an impression whenever and however you communicate. Always make sure that the impressions you are making are positive ones.

On the Side

"Recently a client told us that someone was asked to leave his company because he had sent an extremely vulgar joke to everyone on his e-mail list by mistake. Unfortunately the list included customers and the CEO of the company. Another client told us how someone had sent a message to a coworker saying, 'I NEED TO SEE YOU IN MY OFFICE.' The sender of the message wanted to brainstorm about a meeting they were supposed to have later that day. However, the recipient assumed the sender was furious and was going to reprimand him. It took an entire day for the situation to be resolved and for feelings to be soothed. What a waste of valuable time."

—Image Dynamics trainer

Ask Yourself These Crucial Questions
- What message am I trying to send?
- Is something offensive to me? (Often the things that offend you are likely to offend others.)
- Is the recipient going to understand the meaning of my message?

Tips
If you are leaving a message or writing an e-mail that you think may be construed in the wrong way, have someone read the message or listen to it and give you feedback before you send it.

E-mail

- If you have something pertinent to say or need closure immediately, it is preferable to speak with the person face-to-face or call them on the telephone.
- E-mail does not take the place of a handwritten note.
- Check your e-mail every day.
- Always check your spelling and grammar and proofread the text before you send anything.
- Put the purpose of the e-mail in the subject line and put the action you want taken in the first sentence or paragraph.
- Keep your e-mail short and to the point.
- If the message you are sending has nothing to do with a previous correspondence, don't use the "reply" button. Begin a new e-mail message when addressing a new topic.
- Be careful when you use all capital letters in your message. Most messages that are written in all capitals READ AS THOUGH YOU ARE YELLING!
- Forwarding e-mails to everyone in your address book is not a good idea unless you are sure that all of them need to receive that specific message.
- Sending e-mails with jokes to anyone with whom you do business is inappropriate and shows a lack of professionalism.

Voice Mail
Outgoing Messages

- Use proper English (e.g., "Please leave a message for Kim or me"—never use "Kim or myself").
- State your full name and your company name (e.g., "You have reached the voice mail of Kim Zoller with Image Dynamics. Please leave your message . . .").

- Keep your message short.
- If you change your message daily, update it first thing in the morning or last thing the evening before. Don't forget.

Leaving Messages

- Always state your full name and company name.
- Make your point succinctly.
- Leave your phone number slowly at the end of the message, even if the person knows your phone number. You will get a return call 90 percent faster.
- Write the number down as you say it. This will help you say it at an appropriate speed.
- Use clear articulation, enunciation, and pronunciation.
- Speak slowly so that the person on the other end of the message can easily follow what you are saying.

Conference Calls

- Be on time.
- State your name before speaking.
- Have a call facilitator direct the questions.
- Keep the call succinct.
- Be careful of background noises, especially when putting others on hold.

Cell Phones

- Turn off your phone in all meetings, including seminars and presentations.
- If there is a family emergency, apologize and ask permission to keep your telephone on silent mode. When you answer your telephone, politely excuse yourself and take your call away from the meeting.

- While you are in public, be very careful about what you say. Remember that everyone can hear what you are saying.
- Have private conversations in private.
- Do not text or e-mail on your phone during a meeting.

Texting

- Be careful that you do not use shortcuts or acronyms.
- Read your message again and check spelling.
- When with someone, put down your phone. It is rude to text while having a conversation.
- When in a meeting, people know when you're texting
- Business is business; don't ruin your brand by being too casual while texting. Stay professional.

Faxes

- Call or e-mail before you fax to let the receiver know the fax is on the way or after you fax to confirm that it was received.
- Include a cover page or Post-it note to let the receiver know who sent the fax, who should receive it, and how many pages there are.
- Always let the receiver know exactly how many pages to expect.
- Confidential or revealing information should never be faxed to a communal fax machine. Before you send a fax, find out if there are others in the office who will have access to the fax you are sending. If so, you may want to send the information via a more private method of communication.

Videoconferencing

- Think of a videoconference as a face-to-face meeting.
- Look at the camera as though the lens is the person to whom you are speaking.
- Watch your posture at all times. Use appropriate posture when sitting or standing.
- Do not whisper things to your neighbor. This is rude and will be perceived negatively.

Computers during Meetings

The purpose of many meetings is to build rapport. You accomplish this by making eye contact with others at the meeting. If you feel that you must jot down some notes on your computer, make sure that someone else from your team is making eye contact with others at the meeting. It is extremely important that you:

- Focus on the people at the meeting, not on your computer screen
- Keep your computer off the table unless you need it
- Remember why you are at the meeting (For more information, see "Lacking Meeting Etiquette.")

Big Mistake

8

Using Inappropriate
Dining Etiquette

"The world was my oyster, but I used the wrong fork."
—Oscar Wilde

Many deals are sealed at the dining table. If you are not comfortable doing business over a meal, you may be losing out on a great number of business opportunities. Business dining is about business. When you are eating a business meal, remember that you will eat again. If you know how to handle yourself properly, you can forget about which fork to use and get down to business. Good table manners may not be noticed, but bad table manners will be remembered.

Ask Yourself These Crucial Questions

- What is my main focus while dining and doing business?
- Am I comfortable enough with the entire dining experience that I can focus on the business at hand and not on which fork to use?
- Do I notice when someone else has bad table manners?

─────────────── On the Side ───────────────

"I was sitting with one of my best clients, the general manager of a top Fortune 500 company. He spends a great deal of his time entertaining clients and networking. He ordered a steak and proceeded to stab the piece of steak with his fork and saw away with his knife. I know what *I* was thinking, so I can imagine what his clients or colleagues think when they dine together."

—Operations manager

Tips

You may not be remembered for good manners, but it is a certainty that you will be remembered for bad manners.

Hosting

- Ask the person(s) what type of food they would like.
- If you are partial to a particular cuisine, make sure that your guest likes it as well.
- When you do the inviting, you are the host and you should pay the bill. Vendors are the one exception to this rule—vendors usually pay the bill.

Handling the Check

- When you are the host, arrange beforehand for the check to be given to you.
- Do not argue about paying the bill if the other person(s) insist on paying. If you feel that you should be the one paying the bill, suggest that the other person "Get it the next time."

Seating Arrangements

Allow your guests to face out or face the better view. There are two basic reasons for doing this. First, it is just more polite, and second, it is better to have your guest be distracted by a passerby than for you to be distracted. If you are looking at everything but your guests, they may think that you are not interested in them. Never take the chance that your behavior might be interpreted in the wrong way.

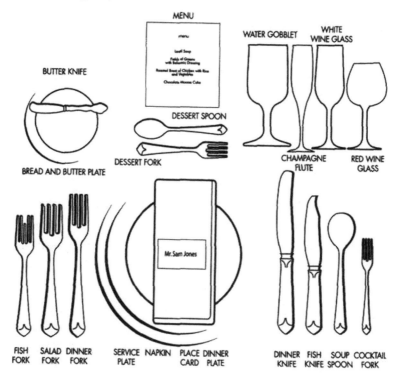

Place Setting

When you first sit down to dine, the table may be filled with glass, silverware, and plates of all different shapes and sizes. If you are at all confused, think of a BMW automobile. The letters BMW are read from left to right. Read your place setting in the same way—starting at the left and moving to the right. Think of the letter *B* as standing for your bread plate, which is located on your left. The letter *M* stands for your meal plate (or your entrée plate) and is located in the center. The letter *W* stands for your water glass and all other glasses or cups for liquids. These are located on your right just above the knives, spoons, and cocktail fork.

Napkin Rules

Once you know the BMW rule, you will not have to worry about which napkin is yours. If the napkin is in the coffee cup and your coffee cup is to your right (with the other glasses and cups), you will know that your napkin is the one on the right.

Remember the following:

- The napkin does not go back onto the table until the very end of the meal.
- If you leave the table during the meal, fold the napkin neatly and place it on your chair. *Do not* put it on the table.
- Do not use the napkin to wipe off lipstick.
- A napkin should be placed on the lap, never around the neck. If a bib is needed (i.e., for lobster or other shellfish), it will be brought to you by the waitstaff.
- When you have finished the meal, do not remove your napkin from your lap. Remove your napkin only when you are ready to leave. Fold it and place it on the table to your left.

Bad Ideas for Ordering

- Long pasta (e.g., spaghetti, linguini, etc.)
- Carbonated drinks
- Most finger foods (e.g., ribs or fried chicken)

Breads

Remember, your bread plate is to your left. Use your butter knife or a clean knife to put some butter directly onto your plate. Break off a piece of the bread that is small enough to put into your mouth in one bite. Butter this piece and place it in your mouth. Do not butter the whole roll or bread slice. It is important to remember to eat only one piece at a time.

Soup

- If you would like to dip your bread into your soup, tear off a small piece of bread and drop the small piece into the soup. Scoop up the bread with your spoon and put it into your mouth.
- If you're eating soup with cheese, cut the cheese with your spoon as you are taking it out of your soup bowl. Do not wrap the cheese around your spoon.
- Move the spoon away from you, skimming the top of the soup. This prevents splashing your clothes. When you skim the top of the soup, you get the coolest part of the soup as well.
- When you are finished, leave your spoon in the soup bowl. If a saucer is available, put the spoon on the right side of the saucer.

RESTING POSITION

Silverware

- Once you use your silverware, it should not be put back on the table, even if a part of it is resting on your plate.
- When you need to put down your silverware, the fork (the whole fork) should go on the left side of your plate and the knife (the whole knife) on the right side of your plate. Both pieces of silverware should cross each other at the top of your plate.
- When you have finished your meal, your knife and fork should be placed together on the plate, with the fork to the left of the knife and the top of the knife and fork facing either 11:00 or 12:00. The location depends on where you are from and the customs used in that area. Placing your fork and knife in this position signals the waiter that you are finished.

FINISHED POSITION

Eating Pace

Watch the pace of your guest(s) and try to finish your meal at approximately the same time. Just sitting there after you are finished may make them uncomfortable, and it may make you uncomfortable as well.

AMERICAN
STYLE

CONTINENTAL
STYLE

Continental versus American Style of Dining

With the Continental style of dining, you hold the fork in your left hand and the knife in your right hand. Cut your food and use your left hand to place it in your mouth. American style starts out the same way, but after cutting the food you then transfer the fork to your right hand and place the food in your mouth. Both are correct; choose the way that is comfortable for you and learn how to do it well.

Wine

Our suggestions are to get a book about wine and to take a course at a local wine shop or college. As a general rule, white wine should be served with fish and poultry, and red wine should be served with red meat.

Dining Dos and Don'ts

- Begin to eat after everyone has been served or after the guest of honor takes his or her first bite.
- Salt and pepper should be passed together. Hold the salt and pepper by the body of the container rather than by the top.
- You may rest a forearm, an elbow, or your hands and wrists on the table. You should never rest both elbows on the table.
- Ask someone to pass what you need. You should never reach across the table to get something.
- Cut only one bite of food at a time.
- Put on lipstick in the restroom. It is rude to apply makeup at the table.
- Use a toothpick only in the restroom. It is rude to use one at the table or as you are walking out of a restaurant.

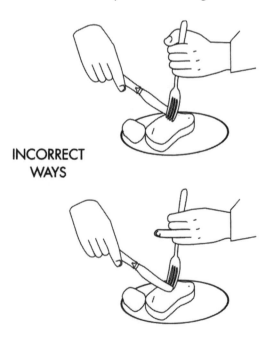

INCORRECT
WAYS

- Bring your food to your mouth. Do not bring your face to the food.
- Salt your food only after you taste it. To do otherwise is seen as an insult to the chef.
- Do not smoke unless your host or guest smokes. In an effort to be polite, many people may not tell you if they disapprove, but it could hurt your relationship if they do not approve of your behavior.
- Do not order an alcoholic drink unless your host or guest orders one.
- Never talk with your mouth full of food.

Gratuity Guide

Cab driver	10–15 percent of the bill
Parking valet	$2.00–$5.00
Room service (if a service charge is included)	$1.00–$5.00
Coat clerk	$1.00/coat
Restroom attendant	$.50–$1.00
Maitre d' (if you have received extra service)	$5.00–$10.00
Waiter/Waitress	15–20 percent of the dinner tab
Sommelier (wine steward)	$3.00–$5.00/bottle or 15 percent of the wine cost (give directly to the sommelier)
Caterer of an event	15–20 percent of the bill
Building doorman (on holidays)	$10.00–$100.00

Big Mistake

Failing to Follow the Guidelines
for Professional Dress

"The apparel oft proclaims the man."
—William Shakespeare, *Hamlet*

People assume the outer package reflects the inner person. Our clothes, our accessories, and our general appearance contribute greatly to the impression we give others. Remember, it is our nonverbal messages that account for a full 55 percent of the total impression others have of us. Professional clothing should be seen as an investment in your future that adds to your competitive advantage. Every work environment is different. It is important to dress professionally for your particular job, while still maintaining your individualism. Clothes do not need to be expensive in order to look professional. Price should never be an excuse for looking unprofessional. There are a wide variety of discount stores, stores that sell slightly worn or used clothing, and a vast number of stores with professional clothes at reasonable prices. It is not the number of clothes you have, where they come from, or how expensive they are that matters. What is important is that they are clean, tailored to fit you, and appropriate for the task. Think before you put on a tie or blouse that has a stain, a shirt that is ripped, or a hem that is pinned. Suits, shirts, sport coats, and slacks should be clean, tailored, and pressed. If you forget one day, that will be the day you run into someone you wish you hadn't.

--- On the Side ---

"I couldn't believe it. On casual day I wore my jeans and tennis shoes like everyone else. My boss came up to me and said, "Nice dirty Keds," referring to my tennis shoes. I didn't think anyone would notice that they were a little dirty. I am now 100 percent aware of the fact that what I wear and how I present myself has a tremendous impact on how others see me. I now really take care of my appearance, especially on "casual day."

—A manager with Nestlé

Ask Yourself These Crucial Questions
- What is my current position?
- What position would I like to have?
- Who will I be seeing that day? If I run into a client, a prospective employer, or the president of my company, will I feel professional?

Tips
- It is important to dress for where you want to be in your career, not for where you are. Usually the people who command the most respect are the people that look as though they respect themselves.

- Remember that your clothing projects your image and has a direct effect on how others perceive you.
- Make sure your clothes fit properly. Clothes that are too tight look cheap, no matter how expensive they are.
- When you buy something new, make sure it fits properly. If not, alter it yourself or have it altered.
- Suits should last at least three to five years.
- Always opt for quality over quantity.
- A coat of clear nail polish daily protects colored nail polish longer.
- Keep clear nail polish with you to stop a run from further damaging your panty hose.
- Save your plastic dry cleaning bags and use them when packing for a trip. This will help prevent your clothes from creasing.
- Take your clothes to the dry cleaner only when necessary.
- Check your clothes for dirt and stains before you put them back in your closet. That way, the only clothes in your closet will be clean clothes and you'll never be embarrassed.
- Your clothing should fit your lifestyle. Do not buy clothes that are just going to sit in your closet. You should feel great in whatever you buy. If you don't love it, don't buy it.
- When you buy something, be sure that you'll be able to wear that item at least ten times.
- If you are a smoker, you should have your clothes cleaned more often than nonsmokers to help get rid of the smell of stale smoke. After each wearing, wash as many items as you can. Note that fabric and hair absorb the smell of smoke, and the odor of perspiration and smoke can make something smell rotten or sour.

Professional Dress for Men

- Your hair should look freshly combed or brushed. If your hair is hard to manage, there are many products on the market that will work well for you. Make sure your hair looks nice all day.

- All facial hair should be barbered or clean-shaven. Beards and mustaches should be groomed regularly. In many companies, facial hair is frowned upon and is not considered professional. Goatees are not considered professional in most corporate environments.

- The hair on the back of your neck should be clean-shaven. When you are getting your hair cut, make sure you remind your barber or hairdresser to shave your neck.

- Your nose and ear hair should be trimmed regularly. You can purchase electric trimmers that make this job easier. Check yourself weekly.

- You may find it helpful to wear an undershirt. Undershirts help absorb perspiration and odor. You will find that they keep you cooler in the summer and warmer in the winter.

- Your shirts should be clean and pressed. Your collars should be treated if necessary. Ask your dry cleaner to pay special attention to your collars since not all cleaners do this regularly. The shirts under your suits should be long sleeved, no matter how hot it is outside. You should have three to five shirts for each suit. White, pastels, and pinstripes are acceptable. Your brighter shirts should be kept for casual wear. Cotton shirts are preferable to cotton blends and look more conservative and professional. Shirtsleeves should extend half an inch beyond the sleeve of your suit. They should never be longer than that.

70

- If you wear a vest, it should fit comfortably and not gap at the armholes.
- Your tie should fall between the middle and the bottom of your belt buckle. Silk ties are best. However, a blend that looks like silk is acceptable. Knot sizes of ties change with the styles. Bow ties are accepted as professional even though they are considered a bit eccentric.
- Keep your ties that have cartoons or slogans for nonbusiness wear.
- Always wear a belt with pants that have belt loops. If your belt is marked from losing or gaining weight, take shoe polish and polish it. If that is not enough to make it more presentable, either take the belt to a shoemaker to have it refinished or buy a new belt. Old, worn-out belts tend to make people look sloppy.
- Your belt should match your shoes. There are belts on the market that are two-toned (e.g., brown on one side and black on the other or black and brown intertwined) that can make this easier for you.
- Your slacks should have a break slightly over your shoes. The back of your slacks should hit the top of the heels of your shoes. Your slacks should be pressed after each wearing. One of the best investments you can make is a pants press. It can save you hundreds of dollars on dry cleaning. Pant cuffs go in and out of style. If you prefer them, cuffs should be kept about two inches deep, and you will still need to have a break in your slacks.
- Wool gabardine is the best fabric for suits. It lasts longer, doesn't wrinkle, and doesn't "ball" up easily.
- Suits, sport coats, and slacks should fit your body proportions and fit comfortably. Have your suits altered

professionally. The sleeves of your jackets should be sewn in rather than stapled or glued and should reach your wrist joint. They should not hike up when you lift your arms. If necessary, have the sleeves altered so they fit you properly. When you cup your hand at the bottom of your jackets, the bottom edge of the sleeves should fall in the crease of your cupped fingers.

- Double-breasted jackets go in and out of style. Look at the people in management in your company and see if other men are wearing them. Some companies do not consider them conservative enough for management personnel.

- Jackets with single vents are more traditional. However, in today's business environments, jackets that have one vent, two vents, or no vents at all are considered professional.

- The color of your socks should match your shoes or slacks. Socks should be long enough so that when you are seated, no bare skin is showing. If you have a problem with your socks falling down, buy longer socks.

- Your shoes should be polished and match your belt. Check for scuff marks weekly. Brown, black, and cordovan are considered the most professional colors to wear. Shoes that look worn can ruin the professional image you want others to have of you.

- Cologne should be used sparingly. If you smell it on yourself, you are probably wearing too much.

- Your fingernails should be kept short, manicured, and clean.

- Wedding rings, school rings, or a small gold ring on your ring finger are acceptable.

Professional Dress for Women

In the business world today, women do not need to look like their male counterparts. Women have many different options for looking professional and feminine. There is one important question that you should ask yourself each time you get dressed for work: Do I want to be considered successful and professional or do I want to look sexy? If you want to get ahead in the world of business, dress appropriately.

General Guidelines

Silk and cotton blouses are best for work. Polyester can be practical because it lasts longer than silk and is washable. If you wear polyester, make sure that it does not look cheap.

Tips

- Your hair should look freshly brushed and combed. Long hair looks more professional when it is pulled back or in a relaxed style. Hair that is heavily teased or in a bouffant style does not project a professional image.
- A small amount of makeup is preferable and considered more professional than no makeup at all. Mascara, blush, and lipstick should be worn daily. Most women look pale and "not put together" without them.
- Make sure your shirts or blouses are clean and pressed at all times and not too tight. See-through shirts or blouses are never considered professional. If you perspire heavily, watch for marks under the armpits. Do not wear shirts that are stained.
- If your belt is marked from losing or gaining weight, take

shoe polish and polish it. If this doesn't work, take the belt to a shoemaker and have it refinished or buy a new one. Often, the "right" belt pulls an outfit together. Belt loops are not a prerequisite for women when it comes to accessorizing with a belt.

- The length of your skirt needs to be appropriate for the style you are wearing, your age, and your weight. A short skirt should be no more than 1–2 inches above or below the knee, and a long skirt should be 2–3 inches above the ankle. You should have your clothes altered to fit your body when necessary.

- Women's slacks require no break. If you need to have your slacks altered, keep the hem the same length all the way around at the bottom.

- The sleeves of your jackets should be altered to fit your arm length and should end at your wrist joint.

- In most corporate settings, hosiery must be worn at all times. It is best to stay with shades of beige, black, and navy. The shade of your panty hose should match or blend with your skirt, slacks, or shoes. An extra pair of panty hose and a bottle of clear nail polish in your purse or briefcase is a necessity in the event of a tear or run in your hosiery.

- Opaque tights are acceptable in cold weather. They should be worn with skirts or dresses. Thin, long socks are acceptable when worn with slacks. They should look similar to panty hose. Black, navy, or brown with no designs are preferable and more practical.

- Try to match or blend your shoes with your clothing. Spectator shoes are acceptable, as well. Shoes that have been dyed to match an outfit are not professional. White shoes get dirty quickly and have a tendency to look old. Wearing shoes that are inappropriate can ruin your entire outfit. Check your shoes for scuff marks regularly and polish your shoes weekly. The heels of your shoes should never look worn. Heel height should be no greater than two inches.

- If you are wearing a belt, it should match or blend with your shoes. Belts that are black, brown, navy, or cream are the most professional looking.

- Perfume should be worn in small amounts only. When you perspire, the scent is doubled. If you are able to smell the perfume after you have applied it, you have used too much.

- Your fingernails should be manicured and clean. Your nails should be kept relatively short in length. Nails that are too long do not look professional. Acrylic nails should not be too thick or too long. Nail polish that is too bright or has sparkles is inappropriate. Nail polish that is chipped or smudged makes a poor impression. Nail art is never considered professional.

- Earrings that are small or medium sized look professional. They should not have a lot of stones or be too glittery. Rings should be worn only on the ring finger or your pinkie. Religious symbols, ankle bracelets, ear cuffs, and visible pierced body parts (excluding pierced ears) are not appropriate. If your ears are pierced, do not wear more than one earring in each ear.

Business, Business Casual, Casual, and After-Hours Attire

Business Attire

Business attire is the most conservative form of dress. It requires a full suit with jacket and either pants or a skirt. When you are meeting someone for the first time, whether for an interview or with a potential customer, business attire is considered the most professional form of dress. The only situation in which you might not wear business attire is if you wear a uniform or have discussed the issue of what to wear prior to your first meeting.

Men

- Wear a starched dress shirt.
- Wear a suit rather than sport coat and slacks.
- Accessorize with a leather belt, matching shoes, and a conservative tie.
- Wear a watch with a leather or bracelet band. Sport watches are not appropriate for business attire.

Women

- Wear a tailored suit that has a matching or coordinating skirt. Conservative dresses that are not flashy, low-cut, or too trendy are also considered appropriate. Dresses with jackets are preferable.
- You can accessorize with a scarf or a belt that accents your suit or dress.
- Your shoes should be leather.
- Wear a watch with a leather or bracelet band. Sport watches are not appropriate for business attire.

Business Casual

Professionalism and consistency are two of the most important factors to consider when you are dressing for success. There is a big difference between casual dressing and sloppy dressing. Do not damage your professional image by looking sloppy. Your dress should be consistent with the image you are trying to create.

Business casual is similar to business attire except that a jacket is not required. Business casual is not what you would wear when lounging around your house, watching a ball game, or shopping at the grocery store. It is one level of dress below business attire but still requires that you be dressed for business.

Men

- If possible, do not wear the pants from your suits as they will get worn out before the jacket.
- Do not wear cotton slacks or jeans.
- Long-sleeved, well-pressed shirts, silk type sweaters, or shirts with open collars and jackets are acceptable.
- Leather shoes and dress socks should be worn at all times.

Women

- Pantsuits are appropriate for business casual attire.
- Slacks with silk or cotton blouses or with twin sweater sets are acceptable.
- Scarves and other types of conservative accessories may be used.
- Shoes that are made of leather, are professional looking, and have lower heels than those that are worn for business attire may be worn.

Casual Attire

Each company has a different interpretation of casual attire. Find out if your company has a policy regarding casual dress. If there are written rules, make sure that you read them carefully.

Both Men and Women

- Find out whether denim is acceptable.
- Cotton or corduroy pants or skirts are acceptable.
- Blouses and shirts may be made of cotton or knit fabrics.
- Casual shoes may be worn.

Many companies will allow you to wear some of the following items, but your choices should be well-thought-out.

- Jeans should not fit too tightly. They should never be faded, have holes, or have frayed edges.
- Shorts should come almost to the knee. Walking shorts or Bermuda shorts are best. Short shorts should never be worn.
- Tight-fitting pants such as leggings are generally not appropriate. They must be worn with a shirt that comes to at least the upper thigh. Keep in mind that not all body types can wear leggings appropriately. It is better to be safe than sorry.
- T-shirts (without logos) must be clean and pressed. Muscle shirts should never be worn.
- Tennis shoes, other types of sport shoes, or sandals may be worn if acceptable in your company.
- If the toes of your shoes are open, your toenails should be pedicured.

Tips

- It is always better to be overdressed than underdressed.
- If it is acceptable to wear jeans, make sure they are in good condition.
- Your socks need to be clean and free of holes.
- If you are wearing a T-shirt, make sure it is not wrinkled or faded. T-shirts have a way of getting the "worn" look quickly.
- When you wear tennis shoes or other types of sport shoes, make sure they are polished and clean. White shoe polish or a shoeshine shop can refurbish them and make them look like new.

After-Hours Business

- Remember, business after hours is still business.
- Women should never wear anything that is too short, too low-cut, or too tight. Daytime suits can always be dressed up with a different blouse and different accessories in order to become more appropriate for the evening. Men always look best in darker suits when they are conducting after-hours business.

Big Mistake

10

Lacking Meeting Etiquette

"Decide what you want, decide what you are willing to exchange for it. Establish your priorities and go to work."

—H. L. Hunt

Leading, participating in, or attending a meeting should always be viewed as an opportunity to exhibit your professionalism. Whether you are a participant or the facilitator really doesn't matter. When people leave the meeting, they will leave it with an impression of you. Their impression, whether positive or negative, will affect whether you work together and, if you do work together, how well you work with one another. It is very important that the message the attendees get is the message you want to send.

On the Side

"A client of ours called the office and sounded desperate. 'What should I do? I just got out of a client meeting and one of our team members took out his nail clippers and started clipping his fingernails.'"

—Sales manager, Fortune 100 company

Ask Yourself These Crucial Questions

- Am I fully prepared for the meeting?
- Does each person have an agenda for the meeting or am I planning to hand out the agenda at the meeting?
- Do I know where to stand or sit in order to have the greatest impact on the others in the room?

Tips

Whether you lead a meeting or are a participant, you must know ahead of time the impressions that you want others at the meeting to take away with them. You need to think about this carefully before the meeting ever starts.

Leading a Meeting

- You must be clear, concise, and articulate.
- The goal of the meeting should be identified at the beginning.
- Each participant should have an agenda. (You may need to send it out ahead of time.)
- The meeting should begin and end on time.
- Do not fidget with your materials, your fingernails, your hair, and so forth.
- Do not put unnecessary materials on the table (e.g., purse, briefcase, coat, etc.). In most instances, a pad, a pen, an agenda, and any backup materials are sufficient.
- Show an appreciation of the points of view of others.
- Have more than the exact number of handouts and preview materials you think you will need. The 5+ rule is a good one to remember: Think about the maximum number of participants you expect to attend and add five more.

- Make eye contact with each of the participants. Scanning the room isn't sufficient.
- Make sure your body language is inviting. People will not feel comfortable asking you questions if they feel intimidated.
- Be careful that you don't give anyone the message that what he or she has said is unimportant. People need to feel that you have heard them, that you appreciate what they have said, and that their contribution is valued. Never argue with a coworker or a customer. If there are areas of disagreement, suggest a meeting after the larger meeting is over to discuss the issue in more depth.

Seating Arrangements

- Make sure that you can see everyone at the meeting without having to turn your head more than 180 degrees. If you find that you have to do so, ask some of the participants to move to other seats. Your team can be interspersed, but the presenters must be able to address everyone at the same time.
- Let the customer know if you will be or might be bringing others to the meeting.
- When the point person sets up an appointment and another team member attends the meeting, it is important that the point person delivers the majority of the presentation. Any changes in this format (i.e., if someone other than the point person will be presenting) require some communication prior to the meeting.
- Introduce your coworkers to your clients.
- If you are in a conference room, remember the seats on either side of the person leading the meeting are considered the most significant.

- Do not sit in cliques, do not break away into small groups, and do not spread out during a meeting unless you need to do so in order to function.

Participating in a Meeting

- Always arrive on time.
- Feel free to participate, but do not participate merely to draw attention to yourself.
- Don't be afraid to ask questions that you feel are relevant to the point being made.
- Before you begin to speak, wait at least three seconds after the previous speaker has finished.
- Do not talk to your neighbor while another person is speaking.
- Confine all discussion to the situation at hand. Do not discuss problems on the side.
- Keep a pleasant or interested look on your face.
- Pay attention.
- Speak up.
- Remember to be clear and concise.

Tips

- Look interested and stay alert.
- Turn off all cell phones and pagers.
- State the ground rules and your expectations for the meeting.
- Give credit where credit is due. Use "we" instead of "I" when appropriate.
- Thinking and planning ahead of time is most important. Gather all the files and materials you feel are applicable

and lay them out ahead of time. That way, you reduce the chance of forgetting something on the day of the meeting.

- If you are dealing with numbers or sales, have a calculator on hand.
- Always come to meetings well prepared. If you are not, you can be sure that others will notice.

Big Mistake

11

Being Unprepared for Interviews

At a glance, Sue didn't think she
would fit into the organization.

"Luck is when opportunity meets preparedness."
—Unknown

When you come to an interview unprepared, be aware of what it may cost you. Sometimes the price you will pay is not getting the job. Preparation for an interview should start the moment you decide on the company for which you want to work and the type of work you want to do for them. You need to plan well ahead of time. Think about what you know about the company, what they think they need, what you think they need, and why you feel they need you. As we've said before, initial impressions are very important. Your attitude, your body language, what you wear, what you bring with you, and how well you present yourself and your information are important to your success. Prospective employers are looking for confident and competent people who can do the job well. Your confidence in yourself and your competence to do the job are revealed during an interview. Being well prepared for an interview can keep you giant steps ahead of the competition.

———————————————— On the Side ————————————————

"We put an advertisement in the paper for an open position and we received hundreds of resumes. We filled the position almost immediately. However, a subsequent resume seemed outstanding. We called the applicant and arranged an interview. We thought, "We need to find a job for her. She's just perfect for our company." She came for the interview wearing a short black skirt, a T-shirt, and sandals without panty hose. If she had known more about our company, we would have spent more time talking to her and we might have given her a job. During the interview she mentioned that she had been on many interviews, but no one had called her back."

—Kim Zoller, president, and Kerry Preston, partner,
Image Dynamics

This applicant had an excellent resume and was very capable and competent. However, she "shot herself in the foot" each time she went on an interview because she was unprepared and inappropriately dressed. It is important to research the company ahead of time. Being unprepared for an interview can be expensive.

Ask Yourself These Crucial Questions

- What do I want the outcome of the interview to be?
- How do I want the interviewer(s) to perceive me?
- What can I do to prepare myself for the interview?
- What will make me feel more confident when I go in for the interview?

Tips

First impressions are crucial for job success. Interviewers decide on your competency to do the job on the basis of their initial perceptions. Remember, 55 percent of the impression you make is through nonverbal means. Have complete control over the nonverbal impressions the interviewer gets from you. Your attitude, your attire, and your confidence in yourself are things that are in your control. Don't give the interviewer any opportunities to focus negatively on something over which you have control.

Dressing for Your Interview

- Wear business attire unless specifically asked to wear business casual. Even if you are asked to wear business casual, make sure you are well dressed and on the dressier side of business casual.

Women

- Suits—Wear a skirt suit or a completely matched pantsuit. You can never go wrong choosing the skirt suit option.
- Blouses—Wear a blouse that is freshly pressed and that cannot be seen through.
- Hosiery—Wearing hosiery is a *must*. Mesh stockings or other types of decorative hosiery are not appropriate for interviewing. Choose a shade of panty hose that is beige, black, or navy.
- Shoes—Wear shoes that are freshly polished and have no scuff marks. A closed-toe, closed-heel shoe is most appropriate for the corporate environment. Heel height

should be no greater than two inches. Black, brown, or navy shoes are best.

- Purses—Use a leather purse if possible. Make sure your purse is free of scratches or scuffs. Black, navy, or brown is best.
- Belts—Wear a belt that matches your shoes or the fabric of your suit. Decorative belts (i.e., fancy buckles, jeweled, etc.) are not appropriate for interviewing.
- Scarves should be color coordinated and enhance the suit.
- Jewelry should not be too loud or showy. Pins should not have a lot of colored stones or be overly large (bigger than 1½ inches by 1½ inches). No more than two rings (with an engagement ring and wedding band counting as one) should be worn. Rings should be worn on only your ring or pinkie fingers.
- Earrings should not be too big or dangly. Wear only one earring per ear. Wearing multiple earrings is not professional.
- Bracelets should not jingle. Ankle bracelets should not be worn.
- Watches should have bracelet or leather bands. Sport watches are not appropriate.

Men

- Suits—Wear a suit rather than a sport coat and pants. Suits should be somewhat conservative. Navy or gray are best.
- Shirts—Wear a shirt that is freshly pressed. White or light blue shirts are most appropriate. Do not wear shirts that have patterns (i.e., heavily striped, plaid, paisley, etc.) or are colored (i.e., bright blue, yellow, pink, red, etc.).

- Ties—Wear a conservative tie (i.e., not too bright in color or with too much of a pattern).
- Shoes—Wear shoes that are freshly polished and have no scuff marks.
- Belts—If your trousers have belt loops, be sure to wear a belt. Your belt should match your shoes.

What to Bring

- Both men and women should carry a briefcase or a portfolio. Leather is preferable.
- If carrying a briefcase, do not carry a purse.
- Keys should be put in your briefcase, purse, or portfolio. Do not put them in your pocket.
- Your resume should be ready for perusal. There should be no stains or creases on it.
- Have a pen and a pad of paper with you at all times.

Your Body Language

- When an interviewer comes to greet you, smile, make eye contact, and use a firm and professional handshake. (For more specific information, see "Using Body Language Improperly.")
- Stand straight and tall. Do not slouch or cross your arms. You want to send a message that you are open, prepared, and ready to get down to business.
- Be energetic and excited about the opportunity.
- Do not wring your hands. It sends a message of nervousness and discomfort.

- Try to mirror the interviewer's position (e.g., if he or she is sitting back, you should be sitting back; if he or she is sitting forward, then you should be sitting forward as well).
- Do not tap your feet or shake your leg. Keep your legs together.
- Do not cross your arms. Keep them in an open position.
- Do not fidget with your pen, pencil, hair, pins, and so forth.

What to Say

- Speak in positive terms. Do not bring up negative situations that you might have experienced in the past.
- Be prepared with at least three questions to ask the interviewer(s). *Never* ask about money during the first interview.
- Be comfortable talking about the research you have done and how it relates to what you will do and how the company will benefit.

How and Where to Sit

- Do not sit until you are invited to do so.
- Do not touch anything on the interviewer's desk. Ask permission to move something if necessary.
- Keep your posture erect. Do not slouch.

Follow-Up

- At the end of the interview, ask the interviewer when you can follow up regarding their decision.

- Send a handwritten thank-you note the day of the interview. Personalize it by mentioning something you discussed during the interview.

For example:
Dear Mr. Jones,
It was a pleasure meeting you. Thank you for taking the time to discuss the [name of position]. It sounds extremely interesting. I am looking forward to the opportunity to work with you and [company name]. Thank you for considering me.

Sincerely yours,
Kim Zoller

When you are interviewed by three or fewer people, write each interviewer a personal note. When more than three people interview you, send the person who was your point of contact a note and ask them to thank the other interviewers for you. Be sure to mention the names of the other interviewers.

Big Mistake

12

Using Poor Telephone Etiquette and Protocol

"When people talk, listen completely.
Most people never listen."

—Ernest Hemingway

Many companies conduct the majority of their business over the telephone. Even though you may not be able to see the person to whom you are talking and they cannot see you, each of you can still hear how involved the other person is in the conversation. Many people think that they are good at multitasking and will work on other tasks while on the phone. Even though they think that other people won't know they are doing something else, other people do. You need to listen carefully to how the person on the other end of the line is reacting to you. Telephone conversations are opportunities to build your relationships. You cannot do that unless you are involved in the conversation and focused on what the person on the other end is saying.

——————————— On the Side ———————————

"I was talking to a coworker who I could tell was not listening to a word I had to say. It was frustrating me and so I decided to have some fun with it. I started saying off the wall things to him and all I heard back was, 'Uh-huh. That's interesting . . .' I realized his attention (or lack of it) discredited his overall professionalism."

—E-Marketing manager
Fortune 500 company

Ask Yourself These Crucial Questions

- Do I get frustrated and insulted when someone asks me to repeat myself numerous times?
- Can I tell when someone is smiling on the other end of the telephone?
- Is it easier and more pleasant to talk to someone whose attention is on me 100 percent of the time?

Tips

Answering the Telephone

- Whenever possible, answer by the third ring.
- Speak clearly and slowly at all times.
- Before starting conversation, state your name and your company name.
- Smile when you answer the phone. It helps keep your voice friendly and welcoming. Keeping a mirror at your desk and looking at it while you are on the phone can be helpful.
- Have a pen and paper in front of you. Always be prepared to take notes.

Making Telephone Calls

- Make your calls early in the day. People are more likely to be available and ready to talk in the mornings. If they are not available, you are more likely to receive a return call on the same day.
- Before you pick up the telephone, know what you want to say and smile as you say it.
- Before beginning a conversation, state your full name and the name of your company.
- Always ask, "Do you have a moment?"
- It is extremely important to get to the point of your call quickly. Be concise. Time is money.
- Thank the person for their time.
- Always confirm when you are going to speak with each other for follow-up. This helps to set the stage for future telephone calls.

Leaving Messages

- You should know what you want to say and how you are going to say it before you pick up the telephone.
- Be clear, concise, and articulate.
- State your full name and the name of your company. Be sure the message you leave is sufficiently detailed so there is no confusion about what you need the other person to do.
- Speak slowly. Many people speak too quickly, which makes messages difficult to understand. It is helpful to write your phone number down as you are leaving your message. This ensures that the person receiving the message has time to write it down correctly. People respond to calls 90 percent faster if they have your phone number in front of them and do not have to look it up.

Returning Calls

- Return calls within twenty-four hours.
- If you cannot return telephone calls within that time frame, let callers know by leaving a detailed message on your voice mail.

Staying Focused

- When you are on the telephone, do not doodle. Doodling takes your attention away from the person to whom you are talking.
- Do not use your computer while you are on the telephone, unless necessary.
- When you are on the phone, keep the number of interruptions to an absolute minimum. Interruptions, no matter how infrequent, send a message of disinterest and disrespect.
- Keep your voice positive, listen carefully, and respond appropriately. Being there and knowing that you are truly listening to them makes people want to do business with you.

Big Mistake

13

Choosing the Wrong Gift

"The man who will use his skill and constructive imagination to see how much he can give for a dollar, instead of how little he can give for a dollar, is bound to succeed."

—Henry Ford

Gift giving in business often becomes part of our jobs. Holidays, weddings, births, birthdays, and other occasions are usually celebrated in the workplace. Finding the right gift for a boss, colleague, or client can be challenging. Whoever said it is better to give than to receive underestimated the difficulty and importance of selecting the perfect gift.

Gifts must be chosen with care and thoughtfulness. The gifts we give as well as how we present them are a direct reflection of us. With that in mind, use the age-old custom of gift giving as an opportunity to make a favorable and lasting impression on the recipient. If your company is paying for the gift, find out whether it has a gift-giving policy that limits expense or offers guidelines. If you are giving a gift to a client, make sure you check your client's policy on receiving gifts.

―――――――――――――――― On the Side ――――――――――――――

"I had just started a new job and a senior colleague gave me a holiday gift. I reciprocated by giving the person a very elaborate bottle of wine. I was so embarrassed when the thank-you letter came back stating how kind, and that perhaps they would put a drop into some special dish they might cook. I can assure you that I always find out what is appropriate before I give a gift."

—CPA and tax accountant, Missouri

Ask Yourself These Crucial Questions
- What are some of the recipient's interests or hobbies?
- How does this gift reflect on my image?
- Will the recipient be comfortable receiving this gift?

Gift Selection

Simple gifts such as candles, paperweights, picture frames, pen or pencil sets, or music are usually best. A gift should be somewhat personal because you want the recipient to know that you gave the gift some thought. However, the gift should not be too personal and should not embarrass the recipient in any way. If you know the interests or hobbies of the recipient, choose a gift with that theme. Gag gifts are not usually a good idea because they might offend the recipient. Another option is to purchase a gift on behalf of a group of your colleagues. In this way, you can brainstorm about gift ideas and, perhaps, increase the value of the gift itself. A charitable donation made in a client's name is a wonderful gesture and is a great idea for those clients who have a "no gift" policy. The amount of the donation should not be disclosed. The honor is that a donation has been made in their name. Choose a charity that you feel will not be offensive to anyone or one in which the client has previously expressed an interest.

Coffee mugs, T-shirts, pens, or other items that can be personalized with your company logo are popular as well. When trying to set yourself apart from the competition, try to pick unusual items that would appeal to individual tastes. For example, a soft briefcase, some golf balls, a garment bag, or a gym bag might work really well. There are many wineries that are willing to private label their wines, using a company logo on the label if appropriate. Gift certificates to new restaurants are a great idea. However, keep in mind that once the certificate is used, it's the kind of gift that is easily forgotten.

Give a gift that fits the individual. For example, giving wine to a nondrinker won't go over well, and a gym bag for someone who doesn't work out doesn't serve any purpose.

Tips

Gifts for Employees

Assistants must be given a gift. The number of years of service should be taken into account when thinking about the gift. If you are giving gifts to other employees in the office, no one should be left out. All the employees should be given an equal or comparable gift.

Suggestions:

- Candy, perfume (make sure you know what scent the person prefers), or scarves

- Jewelry (for an assistant who has been with you for a substantial amount of time)
- Aftershave (make sure you know what scent the person prefers) or ties for men
- Appointment books and calendars
- Gift certificates
- Gift baskets of food or bath products

Gifts for Employers

Employees can give gifts to their employers. The gift does not have to be expensive and should not be too personal. Joint gifts from an entire staff are a great idea. They are less embarrassing for the employer and will cost each employee less than an individual gift.

Suggestions:
- A bottle of wine (if appropriate)
- A gift certificate for two to a restaurant
- A scarf or a tie
- Personalized stationery

Gifts for Coworkers

When exchanging gifts with coworkers, it is important that no one is left out and that no one feels alienated. If you plan on giving gifts to a few people only, do so at lunch, not on company time. Some companies have employees draw a name out of a hat and set a limit for spending. This is a great idea; everyone can be included and the cost is the same across the board.

Suggestions:
- Bath products
- Candles
- Wine

- Cigars
- Ties
- Stationery
- Cooking accessories
- Movie tickets
- Picture frames
- CDs or books

Frequently Asked Questions

Q. Can a gift be too extravagant? What is the appropriate amount to spend?

A. The amount you spend will depend on your personal budget, your previous experiences, and your common sense. If your company is paying for the gift, find out whether there is a gift-giving policy that limits expense or offers guidelines. No matter who is paying, we recommend spending approximately thirty dollars on a classic, thoughtful gift. Food gifts such as fruit baskets, popcorn tins, or specialty candies and business accessories such as pens, calendars, or books are all good ideas. For an extra special touch, have your company logo embossed or printed on the item. Remember that all packages must be neatly wrapped. The gift you give is a reflection of you.

Q. Are there rules of etiquette when it comes to giving alcohol?

A. You should know your company policy regarding alcohol and the company policy of the recipient as well. Some companies prohibit the giving of alcohol under any circumstances. Consider the individual tastes of the person to whom you are giving the gift as well.

If you know the recipient is a wine connoisseur, then a bottle of wine is a thoughtful gift. Alternatives to giving wine or alcohol might include wine books, stemware, or novelty wine stoppers.

Tips

If you are fortunate enough to be on the receiving end the next holiday season, we offer one final tip: Send thank-you notes to everyone who gives you a gift. Nothing beats a simple handwritten thank-you note, sent three to five days after you receive your gift.

Big Mistake

14

Lacking Professionalism
while Traveling

"There are always opportunities through which businessmen can profit handsomely if they will only recognize and seize them."

—John Paul Getty

When you are traveling for business, it is important to keep in mind that you are representing yourself and your company. Business travel is the norm, and the opportunities to do business while traveling are endless. You never know whom you might meet. You need to be prepared for meeting all types of people and for networking with anyone who could affect your business, either positively or negatively.

Ask Yourself These Crucial Questions
- What is going to make me look and feel professional?
- If I run into someone with whom I work or my biggest client, how do I want them to see me?
- If I meet someone who is of value to my business or to myself personally, what kind of impression do I want him or her to take away from the encounter?

─────────────── **On the Side** ───────────────

"I was on my way out of town for a business trip when I remembered that I needed to pick something up from my mentor's house. After opening the door, he looked at me and asked, 'Are you traveling like that?' I said, 'Yes. The seminar isn't until tomorrow so I thought I would travel comfortably.' (I.e., jeans and cotton blouse.) In a serious tone, he said, 'When you are traveling for business, the business starts before you leave your house. What you wear on the airplane, how you look, what you carry, and how you behave all represent who you are and what you do. If someone asks what company you work for, where you are going, and what you are going to do when you get there, making an apology for how you look is embarrassing and, even worse, it is really poor business technique.' I will never forget his advice. I have made some of my best contacts on business trips."

—Sales trainer

What to Take with You
- Briefcase
- Business cards
- Writing instruments
- Legal pad(s) for notes
- Books, magazines, etc., for business as well as pleasure
- Computer and accessories
- Toothbrush and breath mints

Money for Tipping
- Have at least fifteen one-dollar bills for tipping

Airport
- Taxi—15 percent with a $0.50 minimum
- Bags—$1.00 per bag to the airport porter

Hotel

- Bags—$0.50 per bag to the doorman who carries your bag(s) into the lobby; $1.00 to the bellhop who delivers your bag(s) to your room
- Services—$1.00 to housekeeping when you request an iron and ironing board; $5.00 to the concierge will ensure good recommendations if you are staying for a few days—tip each time you make a request; $1.00 to the doorman who hails your cab; $1.00 to $2.00 for housekeeping should be put in an envelope and accumulated for each day you are registered at the hotel even if you don't see him or her

Protocol on the Plane
- Help when you see another passenger struggling with baggage.
- Be courteous, patient, and respectful of all airport personnel; it is not as easy to travel as it used to be.
- Understand that the people who are not on the aisle have needs too. They are not getting up to spite or inconvenience you.
- Greet the people who are sitting next to you. You never know when an opportunity may present itself.

- Talk softly. Remember that others around you should not be disturbed.
- Know your limits regarding alcoholic beverages. Alcohol has an enhanced effect at higher altitudes.
- Assess your neighbor's willingness to have a conversation. Don't assume they want to talk or listen to your life story.

Tips

- Check your ticket carefully before the day of travel. Make sure everything is correct.
- Confirm everything (i.e., flights, hotel reservations, meetings, appointments, etc.) before you leave, even if you have confirmed them previously.
- Store your ticket in a safe place and remember where you put it.
- A good garment bag saves time.
- Put a small umbrella in your bag.
- Take an all-weather coat (with a zip-in lining just in case).
- Travel-size toiletries reduce bulk.
- A travel alarm keeps you in full control.
- Take extra hangers with you.
- Fold shirts and blouses around tissue or plastic bags to reduce wrinkling.
- Line the top and bottom of your bag(s) with plastic dry-cleaning bags.
- Tuck your socks and coiled belts inside your shoes for compact packing.

Big Mistake

15

You Are Your Competitive Advantage

"If you don't have a competitive
advantage, don't compete."

—Jack Welch

Each new day gives you an opportunity to make the day work to your advantage. As Stephen Covey says, "Begin with the end in mind." Each morning, ask yourself where you want to be in your career. Make sure that everything you do that day supports your goal. Don't allow things that could be prevented get in your way.

Challenge yourself daily to exceed all expectations. Remember that you can be whoever you set your mind to be and do whatever you set out to do. If you stay focused, you will become a true professional.

Your opportunities for growth in business are endless if your technical skills and your people skills are fine-tuned. As we previously mentioned, "Luck is when opportunity meets preparedness." Keep this quote in mind as you begin each day and let it be your guide. You—and *only* you—are in charge of how lucky you will be. Your skills for managing all situations successfully, with confidence and absolute clarity, can be powerful tools. If you are prepared for every business circumstance that comes your way, you will find that, indeed, you are your competitive advantage.

About the Authors

Kim Zoller and Kerry Preston are recognized experts in business protocol, branding, leadership development, and presentation and communication skills, as well as customer service and sales training. Together they lead Image Dynamics, the most innovative total-solution training and development company. Both Kim and Kerry are dynamic international speakers who assist individuals and companies with the necessary tools to be successful in today's competitive market. Over the last nineteen years they have trained more than twenty thousand individuals.